GATHERING AND SHARING DIGITAL INFORMATION

MEGAN FROMM, Ph.D.

rosen publishing's
rosen central®

NEW YORK

Published in 2015 by The Rosen Publishing Group, Inc.
29 East 21st Street, New York, NY 10010

First Edition

Library of Congress Cataloging-in-Publication Data

Fromm, Megan.
Gathering and sharing digital information/Megan Fromm.—First edition.
     pages cm.—(Media literacy)
Includes bibliographical references and index.
ISBN 978-1-4777-8062-6 (library bound)
1. Journalism—Technological innovations—Juvenile literature. 2. Online journalism—Juvenile literature. 3. News Web sites—Juvenile literature. I. Title.
PN4784.T34F76 2015
070.9'051—dc23

2014009994

Manufactured in Malaysia

CONTENTS

INTRODUCTION

The hallmark of traditional journalism used to be its gatekeeping function. Journalists and editors represented many levels of information filters, ideally guaranteeing that once information reached the public, it had been vetted for not only its truth value but also its relevance and significance to readers. Now, bits of information and opinion fly fast and furious across virtual communication lines with little to slow them down, except perhaps browser and processing speeds.

In the world today, we literally have access to more available information than can be consumed in hundreds of lifetimes. Some experts call this "information overload." Professor and scholar Clay Shirky has a different definition: "It's not information overload, it's filter failure." What Shirky means by this is that the sheer volume of information available online is not in and of itself a problem. Instead, the concern is about whether anyone, or anything, can help sort and filter this information in ways that are helpful to the average consumer.

Like a sink with no drain and a running faucet, information streams toward us at near-constant rates with nothing to catch the big stuff, nothing to separate out important pieces from the rest of the supply. "Filter failure," then,

We have more information than ever before at our fingertips, but today's digital world often operates without the traditional gatekeepers that help sort out what's most important.

puts the burden of sifting through all this information squarely on the consumers' shoulders. Quite simply, it is up to us to sort out what is real, what is relevant, and what is most important for us in our daily lives and in our roles as citizens of a larger global world.

In some ways, removing the traditional filters of journalism is beneficial—stories that otherwise would not get told, or might not receive significant attention, can now bypass institutional review and go straight to publication online. Additionally, where technology has in part created the problem, technology has also helped devise solutions to this filter failure: aggregation and curation.

CHAPTER ONE

ALL THE NEWS THAT'S FIT TO PRINT (IN YOUR NEWS FEED)

Instead of a filtered information world, we now live in an aggregated or curated news world. Aggregation is what happens when content is pulled from locations across physical and virtual space and presented in a single location. Similarly, curation pulls content from many locations but does so in a thematic or purposeful way, organizing according to a specific topic or demand.

News feeds—or streams of data coded to aggregate and curate news—are now the new gatekeepers. Mobile applications such as Feedly allow users to personalize their news feed by selecting content, which sources to pull from, and even how often to search for new information. Other common aggregators include NewsBlur, Reeder, Digg Reader, and the Skimm, with more emerging every day.

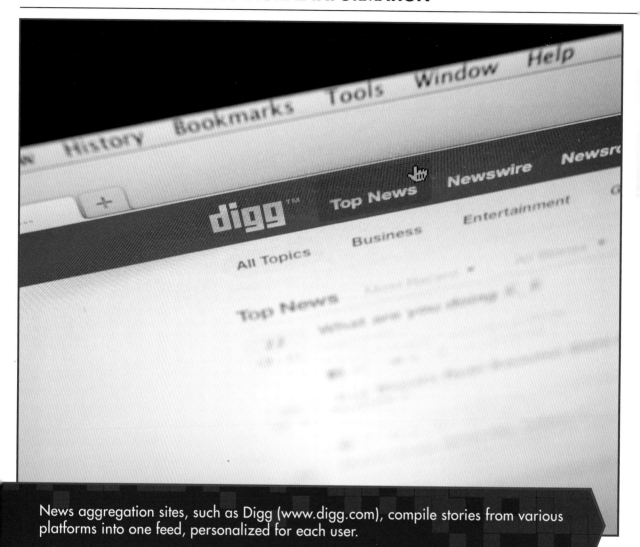

News aggregation sites, such as Digg (www.digg.com), compile stories from various platforms into one feed, personalized for each user.

Another common method of personalized curation and aggregation is through RSS feeds. Standing for "really simple syndication," RSS feeds push content from any kind of website to a user's device, including laptops, tablets, and mobile phones. Whereas other aggregators may push content a few times throughout the day, RSS feeds are almost immediate, sending new headline, story, photo, or video notifications as soon as they are published on the original website.

DIVERSITY IN MEDIA CONTENT

Media literacy requires consumers to be aware of not only the accuracy and truth value of the information they seek, but also whether there is diversity represented among the different views inherent in media content. Without this diversity, we run the risk of perpetuating one-sided, majority viewpoints by consuming only that which we believe and believing only that which we consume. Without balance and diversity from a media literate approach, our curation and aggregation habits become cyclical and narrow-minded.

CURATION AND THE BALANCED MEDIA DIET

Social media sites like Facebook and Twitter also act as content curators. Users deliberately select friends, colleagues, or professionals to be a part of their social network within these sites, creating a bubble of content that is determined by those with access.

More specifically, social media like Twitter allow users to aggregate information in an even more intentional way by offering users the option to set preferences for which people, groups, or trending topics they follow.

These preferences make opting in to, or opting out of, certain types of information so much easier. Don't like what you see? Delete or hide that user. Want more of a specific content? Look for like-minded users who post similar information. This kind of curated approach means we can now personalize our information intake—or information overload—in unique and meaningful ways. But it also means we can easily ignore or dismiss content in which we have no interest, even if that content is highly relevant or timely.

Twitter pushes information to users in 140 characters or fewer, offering a distinctly personalized feed of content.

06

Because of this reality, media consumers who receive all their information from curated sites are likely to be consuming a somewhat limited information diet—a diet that includes only what you want to consume and little else. While this might be fine if your particular choice of entertainment is exclusively vampires or celebrity gossip, it might not be helpful if your choice of news is only one-sided or limited to specific cultural, religious, or political affiliations.

When this happens, as with any diet focused on consuming only what a person wants, balance and health can suffer. In the case of media consumption, an unbalanced media diet full of only certain types of content means other information—the kind that might challenge your beliefs, open your mind, and expose you to new ideas—is left untouched.

CHAPTER TWO

BLOGS AS CURATORS

Some of today's most famous (or infamous) news blogs are really just information curation sites. Take, for instance, *Drudge Report*, a news blog that receives billions of visits per year from around the world. According to BBC News, *Drudge Report* was the first to break news of former president Bill Clinton's encounters with intern Monica Lewinksy in 1998.[1]

But the blog, or Internet "tip sheet," as it was described in its early years, is today more accurately described as a compilation of news headlines from around the world. The catch? *Drudge Report* founder Matt Drudge has often commented that, politically, he is a conservative, causing many media critics and consumers to ask if his blog is merely a platform for pushing that particular political agenda.[2]

Whether these kinds of curated blogs—with no editorial hierarchy, no traditional journalistic structure—can maintain any semblance of objectivity is a worthwhile question. The fact that one man, Matt Drudge, makes all of the

DRUDGE REPORT

PRINCE HARRY FIGHTS ON FRONTLINES IN AFGHANISTAN: 3 MONTH TOUR
Thu Feb 28 2008 11:01:34 ET

World Exclusive

They're calling him "Harry the Hero!"

British Royal Prince Harry has been fighting in Afghanistan since late December -- and has been directly involved in gun battle, the DRUDGE REPORT has learned.

The prince, a junior officer in the Blues and Royals, and third in line to the throne, has been a "magnificent soldier" and an "inspiration to all of Briton."

Prince Harry is talking part in a new offensive against the Taliban.

Ministry of Defense and Clarence House refuse all comment. Army chiefs have managed to keep the prince away from media and have encourage fellow soldiers in his squadron to stay quiet.

Developing...

The *Drudge Report* publishes a mix of content, often linking to traditional journalism sites while also providing its own commentary.

editorial decisions regarding what gets published on his site is markedly different from how a traditional news website works. In the case of the latter, reporters are the first line of editorial judgment, sniffing out stories that might be important or relevant. Editors then help develop these ideas or suggest alternatives if the reporters' initial ideas turn out to lack sufficient news value. Instead, on the *Drudge Report* website, Drudge makes all the executive decisions on which stories are linked, how much emphasis they receive on the site, and whether to add personal commentary or his own supplemental reporting.

For the media consumer who is looking to read a variety of news, the site might look like a useful starting point. Drudge often prints links to stories about science, entertainment, politics, and even sports. The website also provides direct links to other national and international news websites such as the Associated Press, Reuters, and United Press International. But without some additional sleuthing, the average consumer is unlikely to know the background of the website, how it's operated, and the political motivations of its founder.

In short, the media literate consumer can no longer assume that these types of websites—a compilation of links, or an aggregation of news stories—represent a neutral, informed perspective on the world at large. Instead, one of the key approaches to media literacy requires consumers to remember that all media are constructed messages, created by an entity or person for a particular purpose. Now, if we take that a step further and assume that even the platforms or mediums through which these media content are published are messages in and of themselves, then we can see how an aggregation site with a political bent is markedly different from a traditional news website.

BLOGGING WITH A (JOURNALISTIC) PURPOSE

Clearly, not all blogs are created equal, and some can still represent the best in journalistic standards while also offering unique, reader-friendly information. Sometimes, blogging allows those with specific expertise to write about topics they know well and for which they have a wide and deep source network.

Researchers have found that the human voice and interactive elements of blogging attract readers and can lead to higher perceptions of credibility, so in some ways, it is not surprising that blogs can generate a substantial readership even when some professional news websites are flailing. When bloggers take extra steps to demonstrate transparency and objective reporting, they can function much like their journalistic colleagues.

The FCC has declared that advertisers are responsible for ensuring that bloggers adequately disclose sponsored content. However, there are no legally enforceable consequences for not following these guidelines.

written ones. Visual or moving disclosures in a multimedia message should remain on the screen long enough for the average viewer to read and process.

6. Understandable language. Publishers should keep disclosures simple, easy to read, and free from jargon.

The most significant update to the FTC's endorsement guidelines was published in 2009, the same year Ford turned to bloggers to help fuel a grassroots advertising campaign. The campaign, dubbed Ford Fiesta Movement, allowed one hundred prominent social media users to test-drive the Ford Fiesta in exchange for publicity on blogs, Twitter, and Facebook, among other social media sites. The result? According to researcher Grant McCracken, Ford sold ten thousand units in the first six days of sales during the campaign.[5]

These kinds of social media advertising programs are often enormously beneficial for the company because costs associated with the marketing campaign are relatively low while exposure is relatively high. Instead of buying a television ad that might cost $30,000, companies can turn to bloggers and other social media publishers, offer a relatively low amount of compensation via free products or other perks, and make a high return on a small investment.

Because this practice is becoming even more commonplace, it's more important than ever to be able to recognize when a post on social media is sponsored.

CHAPTER THREE

NEWS FEEDS AND THE MOBILE SOUND BITE

Aggregated news feeds, especially those pushed to mobile devices, offer a distinct advantage over traditional publication mediums such as newspapers and magazines: portability. With news and information pushed to a handheld device, consumers can easily use any spare downtime to catch up on world events without having to carry around multiple publications.

Like any technological advancement, however, there is a downside to this level of portability. Some aggregators push only headlines and the first few paragraphs of a story while providing a link to the full source. This means that many stories are only snippets of context, and consumers might be unlikely to link to the entire story. In essence, some news feeds become the mobile equivalent of a sound bite—providing only short, catchy snippets of information and leaving it up to the consumer to pursue additional context or read the rest of the story.

One study of Google's news aggregation site found that 44 percent of visitors to the site only scan headlines without clicking through to the stories.[6] Newer technologies are already trying to capitalize on this reality. In early 2014, one inventor claimed he was on the verge of developing the perfect mobile newspaper: an aggregation machine that publishes news clips in three hundred characters. Blogger Jason Calacanis explained his approach: "We studied what people would want [to read] when they were in line at Starbucks, or walking down the block."[7]

This sound bite approach is increasing in popularity not just because technology allows it but also because it is what media consumers claim they want: short, snappy, clear morsels of information. This instant-gratification attitude toward information is in clear conflict with one of the highest goals of media literacy: to develop critical consumers who are actively engaged in quality, thorough news consumption. Can a person be media literate while consuming only three-hundred-character bits of information? Possibly, but it likely requires ongoing personal assessment of the quality of this information in comparison to other information available from many different sources.

As curators strive to bring in mobile traffic not only to their own software applications but also to the original source of news content, the pressure is on to make headline news as compelling and catchy as possible. In a sense, this makes applications like the one Calacanis is developing a new kind of gatekeeper. Or, as he describes about his own mobile application, "We want to be the place where people decide what to read, not the place where they read."[8]

Only time will tell if this extra step—providing news feeds that suggest and link out to other news sources—will be a media habit consumers are willing to adopt in the long term.

WHEN NEWS "TRENDS" AND THE RISE OF LISTS

Part of what makes news aggregation possible is software that determines which topics are trending—or most popular—on any given online platform. Twitter, for example, keeps a running list of which topics are most referenced at any given time. Other microblogging sites like Tumblr also keep track of the hottest topics.

(continued on the next page)

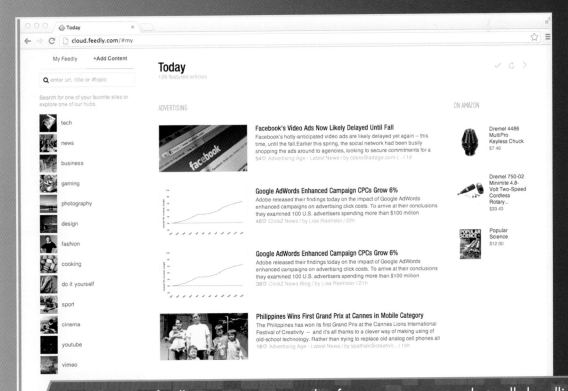

Feedly (www.feedly.com) is one example of a news aggregator that pulls headlines based on user preferences. It can be used as an application on a mobile device or as an add-on to a computer web browser.

(contiuned from the previous page)

This approach is designed to help platform users better understand what others are talking about in the virtual sphere and around the world. However, one look at the list of what's currently trending on Twitter, and users might start to understand the fear that many media users are not exposing themselves to quality content. On any given day, the list of top trending topics might include the hottest celebrities, weather, top television shows, and occasionally topics related to international incidents, such as the Olympics or armed conflict.

Like mobile news feeds, trending news lists run the danger of allowing consumers to feel informed about what's happening in the world without actually exploring a topic in-depth. In part, this shift to instant consumption gratification is even more noticeable in the rise of "charticles," or news articles in the form of quick-read charts and lists.

"NEWS SNACKING" AND PAGE VIEWS

In the last few years, websites like BuzzFeed have made their reputation off articles written exclusively in list form (e.g. "Top 10 Reasons the Political World Is Changing"). While these articles are often catchy and visually engaging, many journalists believe they represent a dumbing-down of Internet content. Additionally, determining where sponsored content ends and original content begins can be challenging to some users.

Using a touch of irony in its article "5 Ways the Listicle Is Changing Journalism," the *Guardian* in 2013 described exactly how the BuzzFeed format is affecting media consumers. Calling this new media consumption habit "news snacking," the United Kingdom newspaper argued that part of the appeal in list-format articles is that younger readers are familiar and comfortable with the style.[9]

Content aggregator BuzzFeed (www.buzzfeed.com) has made a name for itself by publishing information in list format. This method of using "charticles" might provide easy reading, but context is often lacking.

What readers might not know, however, is that information posted in list form—especially when the viewer has to click through each part of the list to a new page—is an easy way to generate more page views, a higher click rate, and therefore more advertising revenue. List format articles are often more successful in search engine queries because the prevalence of repeated keywords helps generate a higher return.

An informed, critical consumer, then, should always question whether these "listicles" or "charticles" are truly providing information, with solid content and relevant facts, or are simply designed to rack up page views.

BLOGGER, CITIZEN JOURNALIST, OR CONTENT GENERATOR

Many people envision blogs as small, in-house productions run by a technology geek or a particularly outspoken freelance writer. While this may be true in many instances, it is not an accurate assumption of all blogs and media curators/aggregators across the board.

Some blog sites, like the *Huffington Post*, are mega-producing content farms with hundreds of bloggers and millions of views per day. These sites often combine user-generated content or personal blogs with links and reproduced material from other professional media publications. And while the variety of content makes these blogs enticing, the extent to which they rely on unpaid submissions may contribute to the devaluation of news content as a whole.

To produce news is expensive—gathering facts and cultivating sources takes time and effort and manpower. In fact, in the digital age of virtual publishing, paying people to actually do the work—that is, to gather information and write it up—is arguably the most expensive part of any journalistic operation. In some ways, the large amount of blogs and user-produced content has distracted consumers from the fact that the end product, a published piece, would normally come at a price. What we once paid monthly subscriptions to access—newspapers—have now been largely replaced by user-generated content that we expect to be free.

This process has attracted criticism in the hybrid blogging-journalism world, and megablog the *Huffington Post* is often on the receiving end.[10] When the *Huffington Post* merged with AOL in 2011, *Los Angeles Times* staffer Tim Rutten wrote about the economics behind the blog's operation. Most notably, he pointed out how these websites, which are sustained through advertising sales based on views and clicks, value the profit potential of a story more than its journalistic value.

THE HUFFINGTON POST

Like many other sites, megablog the *Huffington Post* uses freelance journalists for much of its content. Some journalists argue that failure to adequately compensate freelancers is contributing to the demise of journalism.

Rutten wrote, "The media-saturated environment in which we live has been called 'the information age' when, in fact, it's the data age. Information is data arranged in an intelligible order. Journalism is information collected and analyzed in ways people actually can use." And when users realize that content aggregators are largely designed with high profit margins in mind, they might also finally recognize "an essential difference between journalism and content."[11]

That we now tolerate user-generated content, regardless of whether it is journalistic in nature, to be provided for free to websites that generate multi-million-dollar profits is a sad indictment of how the Internet has changed consumer expectations. In another *Los Angeles Times* story, a *Washington Post* columnist expressed his concern over the trend to not pay aggregation site contributors, saying, "There has to be a concern if free journalistic labor becomes normal and normative in the profession. Eventually that would subvert newsgathering as we know it, and journalism itself."[12]

The "crowdsourcing" trend, which is also known as user-generated content, is full of mixed signals, making it all the more difficult for media consumers to make critical, informed decisions about the content they receive. On one hand, curated and aggregated websites often portray user-generated content as if it were a professional product, and many such sites argue that their crowdsourced content is just as reliable as that produced by compensated journalists. On the other hand, by refusing to pay for user-generated content, the sites inherently devalue this work and imply that it does, or should, represent a difference in something—quality, accuracy, perspective, timeliness.

According to the *Columbia Journalism Review*, crowdsourced content isn't going away any time soon (or likely ever), so news publications should take care to use this resource only when it's most appropriate. In a 2013 article for the *Review*, Lexi Mainland, social editor for the *New York Times*, articulated why journalists must treat user-generated content with the same healthy skepticism that they treat any other kind of information. Mainland said, "I think now more than ever, news organizations—media organizations—should be stepping in to do what they do best, which is

Crowdsourced, free information can provide real-time facts, but it should not take the place of on-the-spot journalistic reporting. Consumers must demand high-quality news and be willing to pay for it.

ferret out what's true and what's real and to figure out what the true story is in a mass of information."[13]

YOU BE THE FILTER

In 2011, author Eli Pariser published the *New York Times* best-selling book *Filter Bubble: What the Internet Is Hiding from You*. The book explains in detail how the Internet's rapid journey to a virtual repository of ultra-personalized information affects everything from citizenship to the economy. Years later, his words still ring true. How the Internet works "fundamentally alters the way we encounter ideas and information."

But his book does more than just explore the many ways Internet functionality affects our lives; he also suggests ways citizens can take more ownership over the information they consume. His ideas represent the core of what media literacy requires of students and adults alike: personal responsibility.

It is no longer enough to recognize the limitations and benefits of a digital age while simultaneously doing nothing to tip the balance in favor of the latter. Citizens who are reactive—or, even worse, passive—in content consumption are essentially complicit in the digital forces that do the most damage to our ideas, perceptions, and place in the world.

To start, Pariser argues that citizens must admit to the need to change our own information consumption habits. By seeking out different types of information and content that doesn't come in the form of a list, and by doing our own curation instead of letting websites curate for us, we may start to experience more of the benefits of information overload and filter failure instead of the downfalls. As Pariser more eloquently describes: "By constantly moving the flashlight of your attention to the perimeters of understanding, you enlarge your sense of the world. Going off the beaten path is scary at first, but the experiences we have when we come across new ideas, people, and cultures are powerful."

Like Pariser, other media literacy educators and activists propose their own methods for combating digital fatigue. Boise State University professor and

With fewer filters and more consumption choices, educators, parents, and professionals are encouraging students to be mindful of their media habits.

Washington Post – Politics, National, World

Sign In   Register Now   Subscribe   Mobile   Multimedia   Today's Paper

NEWS   LOCAL   POLITICS   OPINIONS   SPORTS   Business   Arts & Living

The Washington Post

Hot Topics   Osc

Tuesday, January 25, 2

BREAKING NEWS
Court halts prin

Obama

ongo.tiff @ 25% (Layer 0, RGB/

ongo...

ONGO IS... | HOW ONGO WORKS | SUBSCRIBE

Welcome to Ongo.
Your news like never before.

unprecedented amount of news.
we experience it.

10.7M

Gannett Company, Inc.

GANNETT

▶ **ABOUT GANNETT**
▶ **NEWS FROM GANNETT**
▶ **INVESTOR RELATIONS**
▶ **WEB LINKS**
▶ **CAREERS**

News   Money   Sp

USA TODAY's free i

1 Milli

The New Y

Tuesday, January 25, 20

Search   electric orange checking

1:10 PM ET   **Illinois Supreme Court Halts**

Like developing any other skill or habit, becoming a conscientious media consumer takes time and practice. By reading different publications each day, you can expand your worldview.

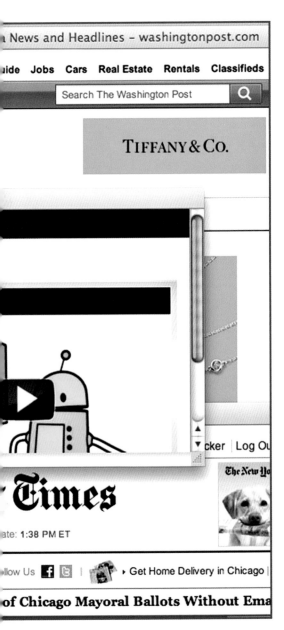

researcher Seth Ashley has distilled much of the focus on media literacy education down to three areas students can emphasize in their own practice:[14]

1. Mindful consumption. Students should be aware of what they consume, their media habits, and how much of this process is automatic or passive instead of active and deliberate.

2. Media system knowledge. Students should know how media operates as a professional practice and as a business. Citizens should understand the subtle ways media messages affect perceptions and worldviews.

3. Individual responsibility. All citizens are responsible for their own choices when it comes to the media they consume and the media they ignore. The pursuit of information requires action and thoughtfulness.

Clearly, the central focus of media literacy is on helping, and indeed pushing, citizens to be more active, engaged, and purposeful contributors to civic life. In doing so, media consumers can become their own filters and curators of information.

CHAPTER FOUR

JOURNALISM, BLOGGING, AND THE CHANGING MEDIA WORLD: AN INTERVIEW WITH JOURNALIST AND BLOGGER AMY BUSHATZ

Employer: Contractor for Military.com
Position: Associate editor, Military.com; managing editor, SpouseBuzz.com
Education: BA in communications, Thomas Edison State College (2004)
Past journalism experience: Intern, the *Washington Times* (D.C.); reporter, the *Washington Times*; staff writer, Politico.com; staff writer, the *Federal Times*; journalism fellowship recipient, the Phillips Foundation; Military.com

Describe a typical "day in the life" of your current job.
On an average day I spend about three hours writing, editing, organizing, and posting content, and an aggregate of anywhere from two to three additional hours interacting on social media or doing interviews. Unlike a traditional journalist who is in charge of one part of the process (writing, or editing, or copyediting, or photo editing, or publishing) I am a jack of all

trades. Blogging means I have to be proficient in all of those tasks. But I rely on social media to clue me into what is happening on my beat.

How do you combat the perspective that bloggers cannot be journalists? What do you do to maintain your integrity or build your reputation?

What makes a piece of writing "journalism"? In my experience it is dedication to accuracy, excellence in writing, mastery of your topic, objectivity, and keeping the interest of your readers as your top priority. Whether I cover a news item on the blog platform or as a hard news piece, I use those principles as my guide. That means grammar, punctuation, and style are just as important on my blog as they are in a traditional newspaper or on a traditional news site. It means that a blog post has to meet the same content standards as any news piece; we seek comment from the people we're writing about, we strive for accuracy in our quotes, we ask tough questions of the government officials we are covering, and we don't just throw words on the Internet simply because we can.

I view our blog as a way to share news in a more personal voice. The difference between hard news and the blogging I do isn't the facts or the standards we meet before publishing—it's the tone we set while writing. We ask open-ended questions, prompt our readers to comment and, when appropriate, insert some of the thinking behind what we're writing. You would never include a phrase like "that sounded fishy to us, so we asked officials what they meant" in a hard news story. But that's acceptable in a blog post. The result of the question to officials makes it into both types of stories. It's just a matter of how it's presented.

My integrity and reputation aren't hard to keep or build. Blogging allows me a platform to cover all the nitty gritty details of my subject the way you wouldn't have space to do in a regular publication. Those I cover know me as an authority on my subject. They know I'll ask the hard questions, demand statistics and budget numbers that they aren't particularly interested in giving, and work my sources to get at the truth. Where I'm posting the news at the end of the day doesn't matter.

How would you respond to those who say you are too close to the subjects you cover, especially when "traditional" journalism etiquette suggests journalists stay more removed?

It's certainly a fine line to walk. However, I am a firm believer that living in the world you are covering makes you a better reporter than you could be otherwise. If you were covering a city government, you wouldn't move outside city limits so that the laws passed by the council or the local elections don't impact you personally. Living my subject matter gives me an intimate understanding of the issues my readers are facing because they are my issues, too.

Do you have a specific code of ethics you follow?

My code of ethics did not change between the day I wrote at a newspaper and the day I started blogging. Truth and accuracy are of the utmost importance. For example, we don't publish information about a person without also giving them a chance to comment. We carefully weigh the cost/benefits of using unnamed sources. We don't plagiarize or "borrow" content from another publication without credit.

Tell us a little about how you fact-check your stories.

I spend a lot of my time doing research online. If I am writing about a subject that I cannot verify with the primary source I link to two, three, or even four other publications reporting different facets of the story who have done so. If at all possible I do my own research, reaching out to officials and their spokespeople and giving them a chance to comment.

Like any publication, there are times when we miss the mark. Social media makes correcting errors difficult because the original story may spread far and wide before you are able to catch the mistake. However, when that happens we do our best to apologize and put a prominent correction into the top of the post in question.

Have traditional media ever published any of your stories in print or online? If so, how did that make you feel?

My reporting is often cited in other publications—both in print and online—just like I cite those other publications from time to time. Getting that nod is a huge confidence boost that I'm on the right track as a respected reporter in my field.

How do you keep up with changing technology and its impact on journalism?

Staying plugged into social media and my network from past employers is key. I keep an eye on what my colleagues are saying and doing. Blogging can be isolating because I do much of it from home, not from a newsroom surrounded by other reporters and information. But if I stay purposeful with my connections, I don't miss a beat.

You write about high-profile political topics and also your own personal experiences with the military. How do you stay objective?

Since I live what I cover, I look at my own experiences as being fuel for the fire and clues as to what my readership is likely experiencing and what is likely important to them, too. As a military spouse and family member covering military spouse and family news, every moment of my day informs what I report. That being said, I do have to take a conscious step back from a subject before diving in and remind myself that this isn't about me, it's about my friends, neighbors, and fellow military family members.

Being so close to the subject can also make it more difficult to cover, in some ways. I have to remind myself that my experience isn't the only one out there. Military families come in all shapes, sizes, and backgrounds, and just because something isn't important to me doesn't mean it's not important to someone else. I use my position as a launching point to listen and understand.

Do you see blogging and journalism as totally separate approaches? How does one inform the other?

I actually see them as the same approach with a different voice. Yes, sometimes we purposefully insert opinion into a blog post where you would steer as far away from that as possible in hard news. But even when we do that, we always do our best to also present the other side. I think that thinking of them as totally separate approaches is how you end up with the attitude that results in examples of blogging not being "real" journalism thanks to sloppy reporting, poor grammar and spelling, ignoring style, etc.

Is there anything else you'd like to add about your experience as a blogger and journalist?

Commenters. Blogging means dealing with a readership that expects you to talk back and yet, at the same time, forgets that you are also a person with feelings. People don't think twice about leaving a cruel comment on a blog post that they would never, ever think is acceptable to say to anyone's face. These armchair journalists are quick to criticize my reporting or credibility as a "real" journalist, but still come back for more day after day. Blogging requires a very, very thick skin…or an ability to let someone else moderate the comments when things get too personal.

AGGREGATION In the context of media literacy, the act of compiling information and media content from many sources and presenting or disseminating the content across a single platform.

CHARTICLE A popular content format that involves publishing a story or information in the form of a visual chart.

CROWDSOURCE To use large populations of citizens and media consumers for gathering information.

CURATION In the context of media literacy, the act of compiling on the same platform similar or related items from multiple sources. Curation is a specific, more purposeful form of aggregation.

DISCLOSURE The act of making known information about products, content, or sponsorship relationships, especially in regard to blog posts.

GATEKEEPER In the case of news media, generally an editor or other managerial person whose job includes deciding which information is published and in what manner.

INFORMATION OVERLOAD Describes the state of having more information available (especially thanks to the Internet) than is possible for a single human to process.

LISTICLE A popular content format that involves publishing a story or information as a list.

MEDIA FILTER A mechanism (either human or technical) designed to sift through media content and publish only that which meets specific criteria. In this case of news media, filter criteria often relates to how newsworthy a story is.

NEWS FEED Often called an RSS feed, a news feed is a constantly updated string of information based on user subscriptions and preferences.

FOR MORE INFORMATION

American Society of News Editors (ASNE)
209 Reynolds Journalism Institute
Missouri School of Journalism
Columbia, MO 65211
(573) 884-2405
Website: http://www.asne.org
ASNE is tasked with helping journalists refine their craft and protect the free flow of information.

Center for Media Literacy
22837 Pacific Coast Highway, #472
Malibu, CA 90265
(310) 804-3985
Website: http://www.medialit.org
The Center for Media Literacy provides many educational resources and
    updated research on media literacy education.

Columbia Journalism Review
729 Seventh Avenue
Third Floor
New York, NY 10019
(212) 854-1881
Website: http://www.cjr.org
The Columbia Journalism Review considers itself a monitor of press across
    all platforms and encourages journalistic excellence as essential to a
    free society.

Federal Trade Commission (FTC)
600 Pennsylvania Avenue NW
Washington, DC 20580
(202) 326-2222
Website: http://www.ftc.gov

The FTC's mission is to ensure that businesses in America operate in a manner that is competitive and fair to consumers.

Media Education Lab
Harrington School of Communication and Media
University of Rhode Island
Kingston, RI 02881
E-mail: hobbs@uri.edu
Website: http://www.mediaeducationlab.com
Media Education Lab provides scholarship and community service aimed at educating students about digital literacy.

National Association for Media Literacy Education
10 Laurel Hill Drive
Cherry Hill, NJ 08003
(888) 775-2652
Website: http://www.namle.net
The National Association for Media Literacy Education is a national membership organization dedicated to helping citizens of all ages learn media literacy skills.

Nieman Journalism Lab
Nieman Foundation at Harvard University
1 Francis Avenue
Cambridge, MA 02138
(617) 496-0168
Website: http://www.niemanlab.org
Nieman Lab aims to help journalists navigate online reporting by providing research and insight regarding journalism innovation in a digital age.

PBS MediaShift
Public Broadcasting Service

2100 Crystal Drive
Arlington, VA 22202
(703) 739-5000
Website: www.pbs.org/mediashift
Sponsored by PBS, MediaShift is designed to be a "guide to the digital revolution" by tracking and commenting on changes in the media industry.

WEBSITES

Because of the changing nature of Internet links, Rosen Publishing has developed an online list of websites related to the subject of this book. This site is updated regularly. Please use this link to access the list:

http://www.rosenlinks.com/MEDL/Gath

FOR FURTHER READING

Ahearn, Frank M. and Eileen C. Horan. *How to Disappear: Erasing Your Digital Footprint*. Guilford, CT: Lyons Press, 2010.

Bauerlein, Mark. *The Digital Divide: Arguments for and Against Facebook, Google, Texting, and the Age of Social Networking*. London, England: Penguin Books, 2011.

Briggs, Mark. *Journalism Next: A Practical Guide to Digital Reporting and Publishing*. Washington, DC: CQ Press, 2010.

Brock, George. *Out of Print: Newspapers, Journalism, and the Business of News in the Digital Age*. London, England: Kogan Page Limited, 2013.

Hobbs, Renee. *Digital and Media Literacy: Connecting Culture and Classroom*. Thousand Oaks, CA: Corwin, 2011.

Jenkins, Henry. *Convergence Culture: Where Old & New Media Collide*. New York, NY: New York University, 2006.

Jenkins, Henry. *Spreadable Media: Creating Value and Meaning in a Networked Culture*. New York, NY: New York University Press, 2013.

Johnson, Clay. *The Information Diet: A Case for Conscious Consumption*. Cambridge, MA: O'Reilly, 2011.

Jones, Alex. *Losing the News: The Future of the News that Feeds Democracy*. New York: Oxford University Press, 2009.

Kaye, Jeff. *Funding Journalism in the Digital Age: Business Models, Strategies, Issues, and Trends*. New York, NY: Peter Lang, 2010.

Kovach, Bill, and Tom Rosenstiel. *Blur: How to Know What's True in the Age of Information Overload*. New York, NY: Bloomsbury, 2010.

Mayor-Schonberger, Viktor, and Kenneth Cukier. *Big Data: A Revolution that Will Transform How We Live, Work, and Think*. New York, NY: Houghton Mifflin Harcourt, 2013.

Reimold, Daniel. *Journalism of Ideas: Brainstorming, Developing, and Selling Stories in the Digital Age*. New York, NY: Routledge Publishing, 2013.

Rosenbaum, Steven. *Curation Nation: How to Win in a World Where Consumers Are Creators*. New York, NY: McGraw Hill, 2011.

END NOTES

[1] BBC News. "Scandalous Scoop Breaks Online." January 25, 1998. Retrieved February 19, 2014 (http://news.bbc.co.uk/2/hi/special_report/1998/clinton_scandal/50031.stm).

[2] Sokol, Brett. "The Drudge Retort." *Miami New Times*, June 28, 2001. Retrieved February 21, 2014 (http://www.miaminewtimes.com/2001-06-28/news/the-drudge-retort).

[3] Hawkins, Sara. "What Marketers Need to Know About the New FTC Disclosures." *Social Media Examiner*, May 1, 2013. Retrieved March 1, 2014 (http://www.socialmediaexaminer.com/ftc-2013-disclosures).

[4] Federal Trade Commission. ".com Disclosures: How to Make Effective Disclosures in Digital Advertising." 2013. Retrieved March 2, 2014 (http://www.ftc.gov/sites/default/files/attachments/press-releases/ftc-staff-revises-online-advertising-disclosure-guidelines/130312dotcomdisclosures.pdf).

[5] McCracken, Grant. "How Ford Got Social Marketing Right." *Harvard Business Review*, January 7, 2010. Retrieved February 19, 2014 (http://blogs.hbr.org/2010/01/ford-recently-wrapped-the-firs).

[6] Wauters, Robin. "Report: 44% of Google News Visitors Scan Headlines, Don't Click Through." *TechCrunch*, January 19, 2010. Retrieved February 24, 2014 (http://techcrunch.com/2010/01/19/outsell-google-news).

[7] Ingraham, Nathan. "All in an Update: Inside App Aims to Be the Perfect Mobile Newspaper." *The Verge*, January 28, 2014. Retrieved February 21, 2014 (http://www.theverge.com/2014/1/28/5352440/inside-app-aims-to-be-the-perfect-mobile-newspaper).

[8] Ingraham, Nathan. "All in an Update."

[9] Lawlor, Anna. "5 Ways the Listicle Is Changing Journalism." *Guardian*, August 12, 2013. Retrieved February 27, 2014 (http://www.theguardian.com/media-network/media-network-blog/2013/aug/12/5-ways-listicle-changing-journalism).

[10] Rutten, Tim. "AOL? HuffPo. The Loser? Journalism." *Los Angeles Times*, February 9, 2011. Retrieved February 27, 2014 (http://articles.latimes.

com/2011/feb/09/opinion/la-oe-rutten-column-huffington-aol-20110209).

[11] Silver, Nate. "The Economics of Blogging and the Huffington Post." *New York Times*, February 12, 2011. Retrieved February 27, 2014 (http://fivethirtyeight.blogs.nytimes.com/2011/02/12/the-economics-of-blogging-and-the-huffington-post/?_php=true&_type=blogs&_r=0).

[12] Rainey, James. "On the Media: The Price of 'Free' Journalism." *Los Angeles Times*, May 14, 2011. Retrieved February 24, 2014 (http://articles.latimes.com/2011/may/14/entertainment/la-et-onthemedia-20110514).

[13] Akagi, Katie, and Stephanie Linning. "Crowdsourcing Done Right." *Columbia Journalism Review*, April 29, 2013. Retrieved February 25, 2014 (http://www.cjr.org/data_points/crowdsourcing_done_right.php?page=2).

[14] Ashley, Seth. "Teaching Nuance: The Need for Media Literacy in the Digital Age." *Blue Review*, 2013. Retrieved February 27, 2014 (http://thebluereview.org/teaching-media-literacy).

INDEX

ABOUT THE AUTHOR

Megan Fromm is an assistant professor at Boise State University and faculty for the Salzburg Academy on Media & Global Change, a summer media literacy study-abroad program. She is also the professional support director for the Journalism Education Association.

Fromm received her Ph.D. in 2010 from the Philip Merrill College of Journalism at the University of Maryland. Her dissertation analyzed how news media frame student First Amendment court cases, particularly those involving freedom of speech and press. Her work and teaching centers on media law, scholastic journalism, media literacy, and media and democracy. She has also worked as a journalist and high school journalism teacher. Fromm has taught at Johns Hopkins University, Towson University, the University of Maryland, and the Newseum.

As a working journalist, Fromm won numerous awards, including the Society of Professional Journalists Sunshine Award and the Colorado Friend of the First Amendment Award. Fromm worked in student media through high school and college and interned at the Student Press Law Center in 2004. Her career in journalism began at Grand Junction High School (Grand Junction, Colorado), where she was a reporter and news editor for the award-winning student newspaper, the *Orange & Black*.

PHOTO CREDITS